Everybody's family is special and unique.
Your family is special and unique.

How Many Grown-ups Do You Have?
Copyright © 2023 by Polina Buchan

Second edition 2023

ISBN: 978-1-7390506-0-3
Independently published

Kai lives with their Gramma, Grampa and Mom. Kai's family loves taking their dog Biscuit for walks together. Kai is 7 years old, and they have 3 grown-ups: Gramma, Grampa, and Mom.

Mala has 2 dads: Dad and Papa. Dad and Papa used to live together, but they don't anymore. Dad now lives with his partner Alex, and Papa lives alone. Mala has 3 grown-ups: Dad, Papa and Alex.

Niko has 2 dads as well.
Niko lives with Dad and Daddy.
Niko also spends time with Ali.
Ali gave birth to Niko so that Dad
and Daddy could have a baby.
Ali and Niko meet up at the park
and have ice cream.
Niko has 3 grown ups.

Sunita and her dad, whom she calls Appa, live in an apartment. Appa picks Sunita up from school. She reads while he makes dinner.
Sunita loves Appa's cooking. She has 1 grown-up.

Nina lives with Papa, Mama and
Kate. Together, they are a family.
They like to have dance parties
in the living room. Papa, Mama
and Kate love each other, and
they all love Nina very much.
Nina has 3 grown-ups.

Rory and Morgan are siblings.
They live with Mommy.
Mommy's partner Amira comes
to visit. They go outside and fly a
kite together. Rory and Morgan
have 2 grown-ups.

JUNE

Oscar's parents have separate homes. Some weeks, Oscar lives with Mom in her house, where he has a cat! Other weeks, Oscar lives with Dad in his apartment, where he has his own room! Oscar has 2 grown-ups.

Briar has 4 grown-ups: Papa, Dad, Mommy, and Nora. All of them live together. On Saturdays, they go to the library and bring home new books. Briar loves having 4 grown-ups. There is always someone to read with!

Imani has 2 moms: Mama and Mommy. Mama and Mommy adopted Imani when she was a baby. Now they all live together on the farm. Imani helps take care of the chickens and feeds the goats. She has 2 grown-ups: Mama and Mommy.

Quinn is 11 years old. They live with Dad, but stay at Mom and Stepdad's house on weekends. Mom and Stepdad have a new baby, Lyla. Quinn loves their half-sister Lyla very much. Quinn has **3** grown-ups: Dad, Mom and Stepdad.

Alex lives in a foster home with their Foster Parents Kathy and Igor. Some day, Alex might live with Papa, but it is not possible right now. Papa comes to visit Alex at the foster home.
For now, Alex has 3 grown-ups: Kathy, Igor and Papa.

Isabella and Edgar are siblings. They live with their whole family. Isabella and Edgar have 5 grown-ups: Mami, Papá, Tío Luis, Abuelo and Abuela. Every Friday, they all have a family dinner together. There is so much love in this big house!

Some kids have 1 grown-up.
Some kids have 2.
Some have 3.
Some have 4.
Some have 5 or more.

Some kids have 1 mom.
Some kids have 2 dads.
Some kids have 3 parents.
Some kids live with grandparents.
Some kids don't have parents.

Some kids are cared for
by different grown-ups
at different times.

Some kids live with their
grown-ups, and some don't.

How many
grown-ups do
YOU have?

Visit www.polinabuchan.com for free printable resources, worksheets and colouring pages to accompany this book!

Additional Reading: Family Vocabulary!

- **LGBTQ+** stands for lesbian, gay, bisexual, transgender, queer, plus other people who use different language to describe a variety of identities. For example, Mala's Dad and Papa are part of the LGBTQ+ community, as are many other people in this book.
- **Transgender** people identify with a different gender from the one they were assigned at birth.
- **Non-binary, genderqueer and genderfluid** are some of the terms used by people who don't identify specifically as a man or a woman. Everyone's gender and how they feel about themselves is unique to them, and we can't tell a person's gender just by looking at them. Kai is non-binary and uses the pronoun "they".
- **Polyamorous** people love more than one person at a time. Sometimes that means that multiple adults, some or all of whom are in a loving relationship, live together, like Briar's 4 grown-ups. And sometimes adults date multiple people, but don't live with them.
- **Co-parents** are parents who usually don't live together but work as a team to care for their child. Sometimes that means that the child has more than one home. Oscar's parents are co-parenting, and Oscar has two homes.
- **Stepparents** are partners of a kid's parents who also care for the kid. Not all partners are called Stepparents, but it's a common word. Quinn's Mom has a new partner, who Quinn calls Stepdad.
- **Stepsiblings** (stepbrothers, stepsisters) are children who become siblings when their parents marry, but they do not share a biological parent. If two children share one biological parent, like Quinn and baby Lyla who have the same Mom, they are **half-siblings** (half-brothers, half-sisters).
- **Surrogate** is a person who carries and gives birth to a baby for a person who is not able to have children. Niko's Dad and Daddy couldn't have a baby on their own, and they asked Ali to grow a baby for them in her belly.
- **Adoption** happens when a kid is not raised by their birth parents, but joins a new family, who raise the child as their own. Mama and Mommy are Imani's adoptive parents. Imani joined their family when she was a baby, but kids can be adopted when they are older, too.
- **Foster homes** are temporary homes for children who don't currently live with their parents. Foster children are cared for by foster parents. Children stay with a foster family until they can reunite with their parents, or until they are adopted. Alex's foster parents are Kathy and Igor, and Papa is Alex's parent.

About the author and illustrator:

Polina Buchan is a Canadian children's author, professor and mama.
She mainly writes books for curious toddlers, and also enjoys playing
with watercolour paint. Polina is passionate about showcasing inclusive
language and diversity in her work. Polina's books aim to engage the
youngest of readers on a variety of (sometimes complex) topics in a
simple and direct way.

About this book:

"Like many children, my daughter has a family that some might call
unique or unconventional. In a queer, non-traditional household, whose
polyamorous dynamic is hard to summarize in one sentence, my child is
surrounded by love and support from her three grown-ups. Although
this may at first glance appear "unusual", my daughter is far from the
only one with a non-nuclear family that includes three, four or more
adults or parent-figures! Queer families of various configurations,
multi-generational families, single-parent families, co-parenting
families, adoptive families, step-families, foster families and many
other "non-traditional" families are all around us, but, unfortunately,
still under-represented in children's literature. Polyamorous families, in
particular, are almost non-existent in content for the very youngest of
readers.
I first created this book to help my toddler see that her family is both
unique AND not-so-uncommon. I thought that this resource could also
help other families to start conversations about the beautiful diversity
of families." - Polina

More from Canadian children's author Polina Buchan:

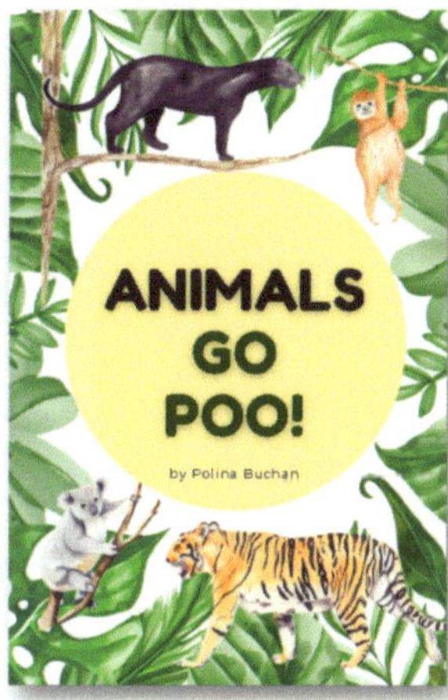

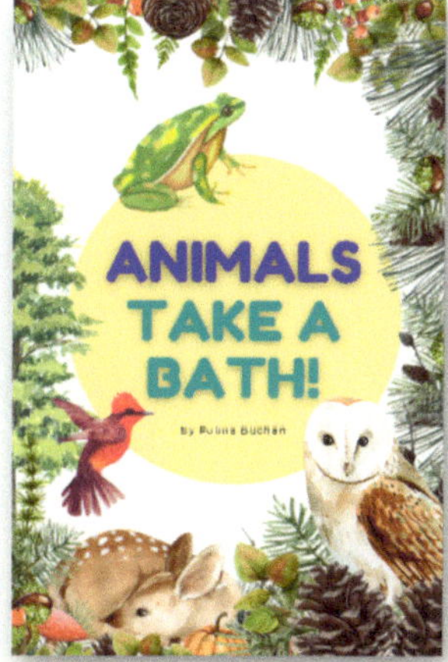

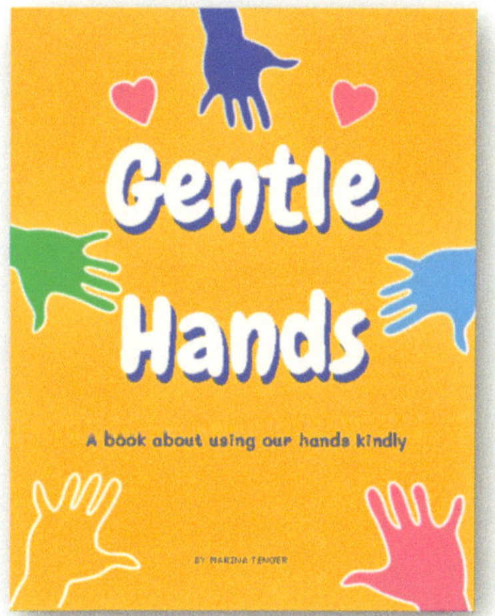

www.polinabuchan.com
or search on Amazon